Learn with Me: Ready to Read

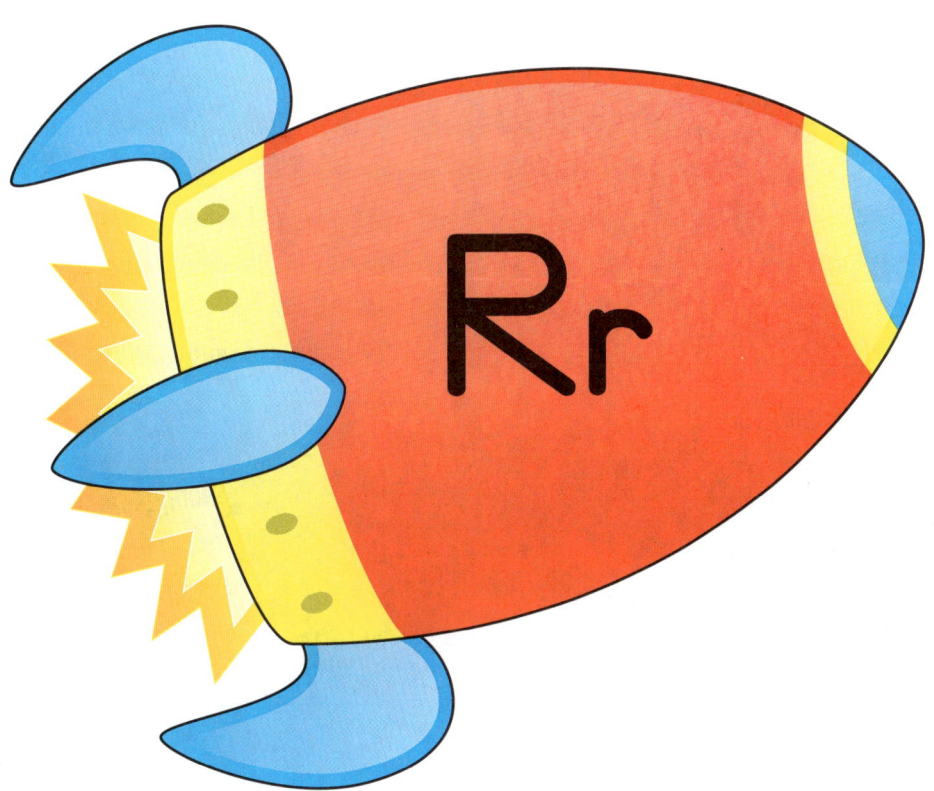

Carson-Dellosa Publishing LLC
Greensboro, North Carolina

Credits

Content Editor: Joanie Oliphant

Copy Editor: Jesse Koziol

Layout Design: Lori Jackson

Spectrum
An imprint of Carson-Dellosa Publishing LLC
PO Box 35665
Greensboro, NC 27425 USA
carsondellosa.com

© 2011, Carson-Dellosa Publishing LLC. Except as permitted under the United States Copyright Act, no part of this publication may be reproduced, stored, or distributed in any form or by any means (mechanically, electronically, recording, etc.) without the prior written consent of Carson-Dellosa Publishing LLC. Spectrum is an imprint of Carson-Dellosa Publishing LLC.

Printed in the USA • All rights reserved.

ISBN 978-1-936024-77-3
06-189197811

Table of Contents

Introduction 4
A Is for Apple 5
Aa 6
B Is for Butterfly 7
Bb 8
C Is for Car 9
Cc 10
Matching Pictures with
    the Sounds of B and C 11
D Is for Dinosaur 13
Dd 14
E Is for Elephant 15
Ee 16
F Is for Fish 17
Ff 18
Matching Pictures with
    the Sounds of D and F 19
G Is for Gift 21
Gg 22
H Is for House 23
Hh 24
Matching Pictures with
    the Sounds of G and H 25
I Is for Ice Cream 27
Ii 28
J Is for Jellyfish 29
Jj 30
K Is for Kangaroo 31
Kk 32
Matching Pictures with
    the Sounds of J and K 33
L Is for Ladybug 35
Ll 36
M Is for Mouse 37
Mm 38
Matching Pictures with
    the Sounds of L and M 39
N Is for Newt 41
Nn 42

O Is for Octopus 43
Oo 44
P Is for Penguin 45
Pp 46
Matching Pictures with
    the Sounds of N and P 47
Q Is for Quail 49
Qq 50
R Is for Rabbit 51
Rr 52
S Is for Sun 53
Ss 54
Matching Pictures with
    the Sounds of R and S 55
T Is for Turtle 57
Tt 58
U Is for Umbrella 59
Uu 60
V Is for Vulture 61
Vv 62
Matching Pictures with
    the Sounds of T and V 63
W Is for Walrus 65
Ww 66
X Is for Fox 67
Xx 68
Y Is for Yak 69
Yy 70
Z Is for Zebra 71
Zz 72
Matching Pictures with
    the Sounds of W, Y, and Z ... 73
Word and Number
    Matching Game 75
Color Matching Game 77
All About Me 79

© Carson-Dellosa

Introduction

Welcome to *Learn with Me: Ready to Read*. You and your child are about to start on a new adventure. Research tells us that children whose parents help prepare them for reading are more likely to develop a range of literacy skills, including the abilities to listen, speak, read, and write. Holding books, turning pages, looking at illustrations, and enjoying the experience of being read to by an adult are among the first steps to literacy development. During these activities, children also begin to associate reading with pleasurable experiences.

Reading and writing develop simultaneously. Young children begin to develop early reading behaviors when they notice that symbols have meaning. When a child calls out the name of a favorite restaurant or store upon seeing its sign, the child is demonstrating an early reading skill. Scribbling on paper and write-on/wipe-away boards is an early writing skill. A child who observes a family member writing a grocery list may write on a sheet of paper and take the "list" to the store. These attempts to understand and use written language are the foundation of literacy development. The child will add skills such as associating letters with their sounds and accurately forming letters and words to become a reader and writer.

The focus of *Learn with Me: Ready to Read* is to help your child recognize and write uppercase and lowercase letters. It also offers the opportunity for your child to learn common consonant and vowel sounds of the letters. A hidden picture of an animal or an object is used to present the uppercase and lowercase form of each letter. Your child will then practice tracing and writing the letters. The phonetic sound of the letter is then introduced with pictures. After naming the pictures, encourage your child to think of other words that start with the same sound. You might even play a game with riddles to help your child think of additional words. For example, when learning the *b* sound you might say, "I am thinking of an insect that flies from flower to flower. What is it?"

It is not necessary to teach letter concepts in alphabetical order. Some letters such as *b*, *d*, *f*, *l*, *m*, *p*, *s*, and *t* have clear, easy-to-pronounce sounds. They may be good choices for starting out. Others, such as *c*, *g*, *n*, and *x*, may have more than one sound or be more difficult for a child to say. Therefore, it may be more helpful to begin with a letter that has a clear sound. Another good approach might be to begin with the first letter of your child's name or with a letter associated with a picture that interests your child.

As you work, focus on having fun and on the excitement your child feels upon learning the letter names and sounds. You will be spending your time in the valuable pursuit of developing pre-reading skills that result in increased kindergarten readiness.

Enjoy learning together!

The Spectrum Team

A Is for Apple

Directions: Color the spaces with **A** red. Color the spaces with **a** blue.

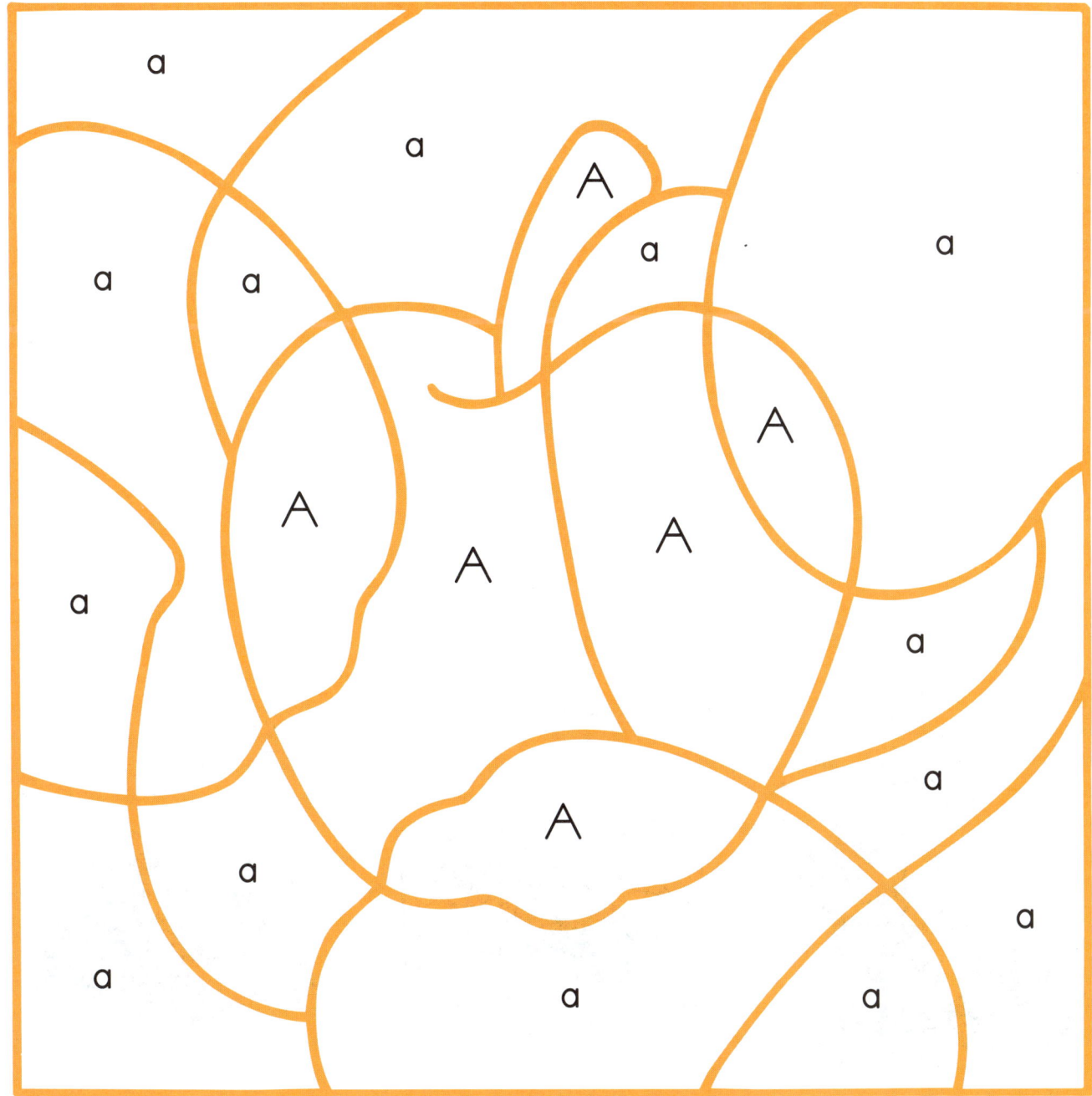

Aa

Directions: Trace and write the letters. Use the blank line for extra practice.

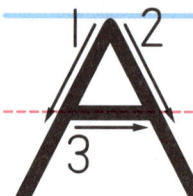

These words have the short **a** sound. Write the letter **a** on the lines.

   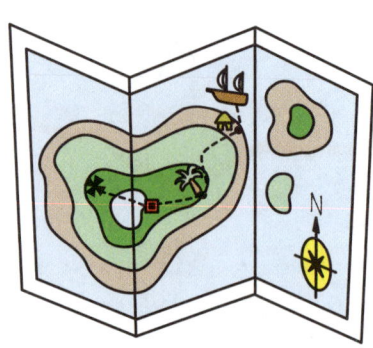   

__nt   m__p   h__t

B Is for Butterfly

Directions: Color the spaces with B red. Color the spaces with b yellow.

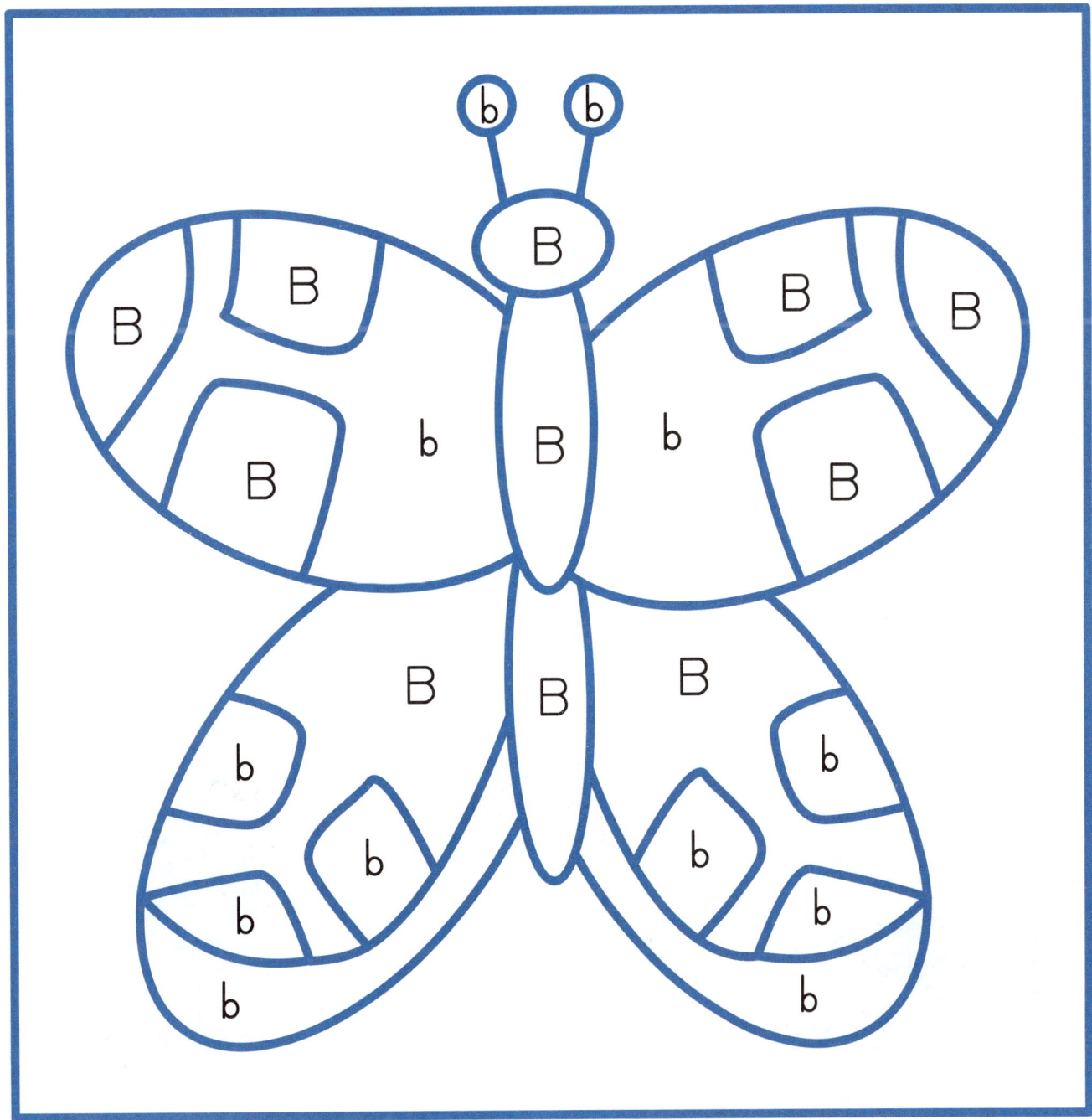

Bb

Directions: Trace and write the letters. Use the blank line for extra practice.

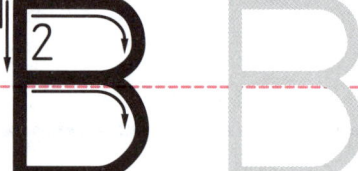

These words start with the letter **b**. Write **b** on the lines.

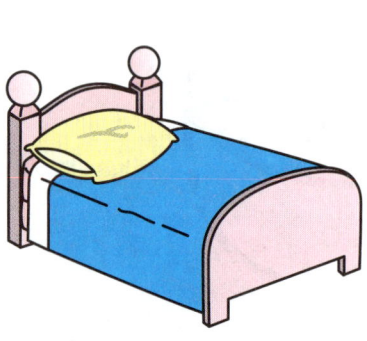   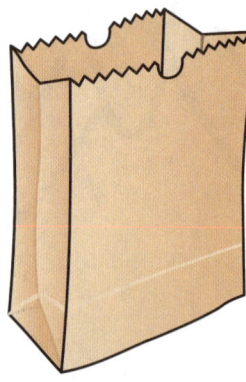   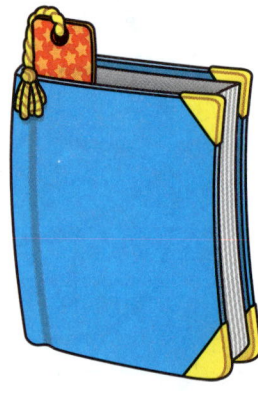

___ed   ___ag   ___ook

C Is for Car

Directions: Color the spaces with C blue. Color the spaces with c green.

Cc

Directions: Trace and write the letters. Use the blank line for extra practice.

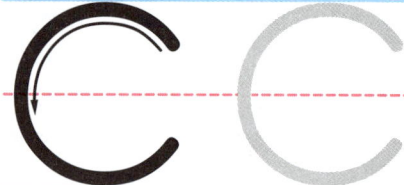

These words start with the letter **c**. Write **c** on the lines.

___ow   ___up   ___at

Matching Pictures with the Sounds of B and C

Directions: Cut apart the pictures. Place the pictures that start with **Bb** on the ball. Place the pictures that start with **Cc** on the cup.

cut

D Is for Dinosaur

Directions: Color the spaces with D orange. Color the spaces with d purple.

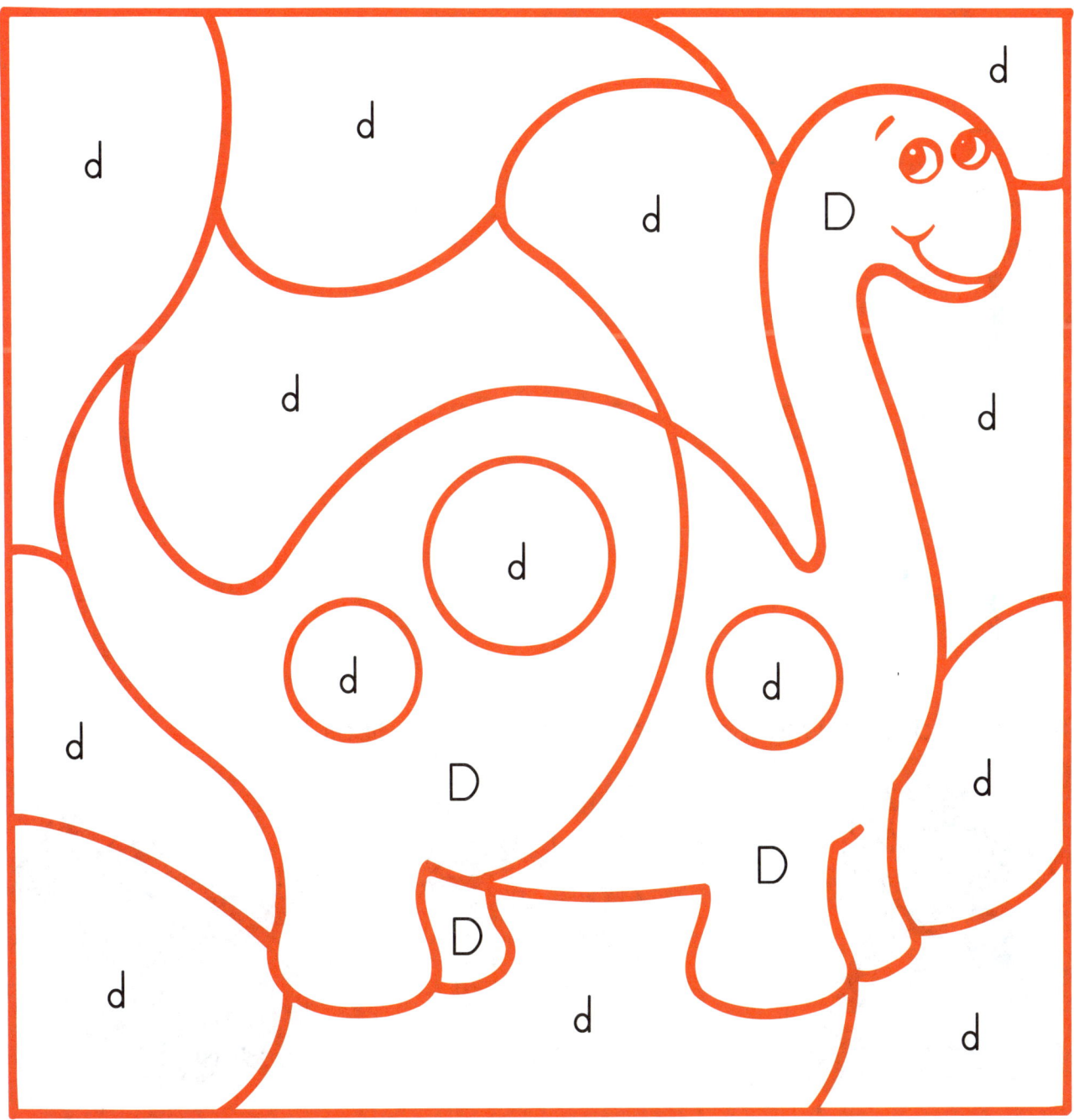

Dd

Directions: Trace and write the letters. Use the blank line for extra practice.

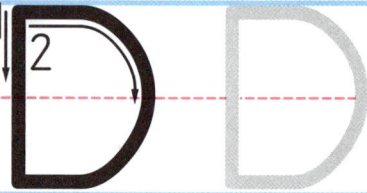

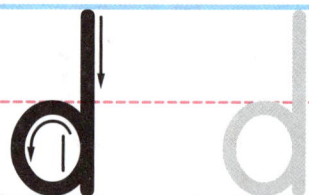

These words start with the letter **d**. Write **d** on the lines.

___oll   ___uck   ___og

E Is for Elephant

Directions: Color the spaces with E gray. Color the spaces with e pink.

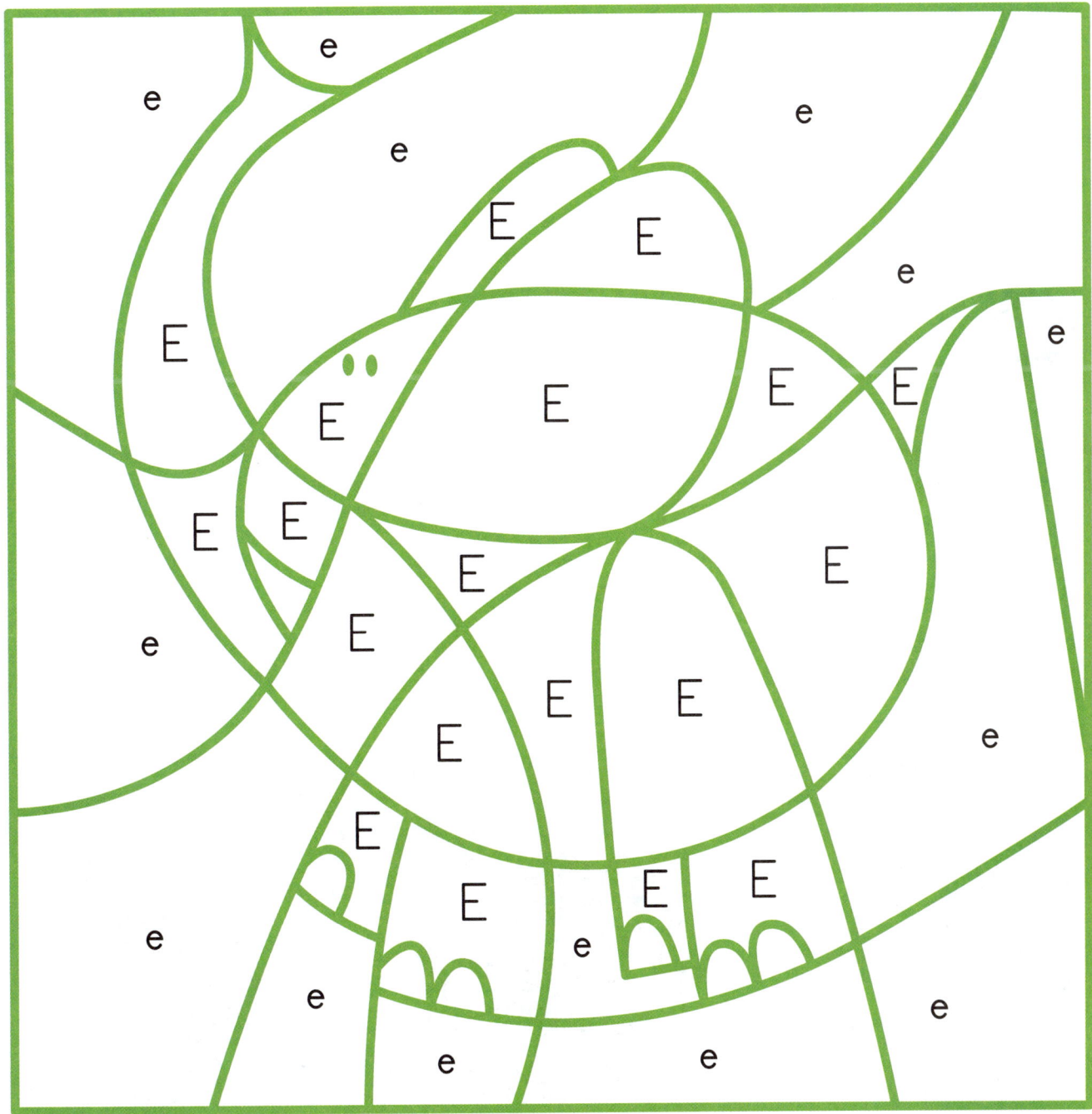

© Carson-Dellosa

Ee

Directions: Trace and write the letters. Use the blank line for extra practice.

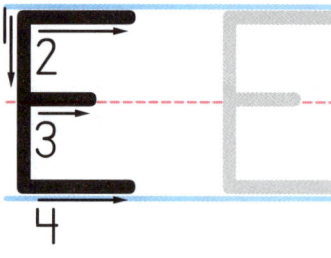

These words have the short **e** sound. Write the letter **e** on the lines.

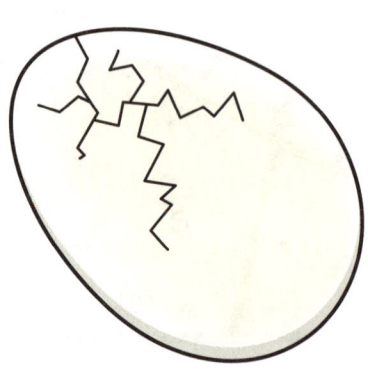  

___gg   w___b   h___n

F Is for Fish

Directions: Color the spaces with F blue. Color the spaces with f orange.

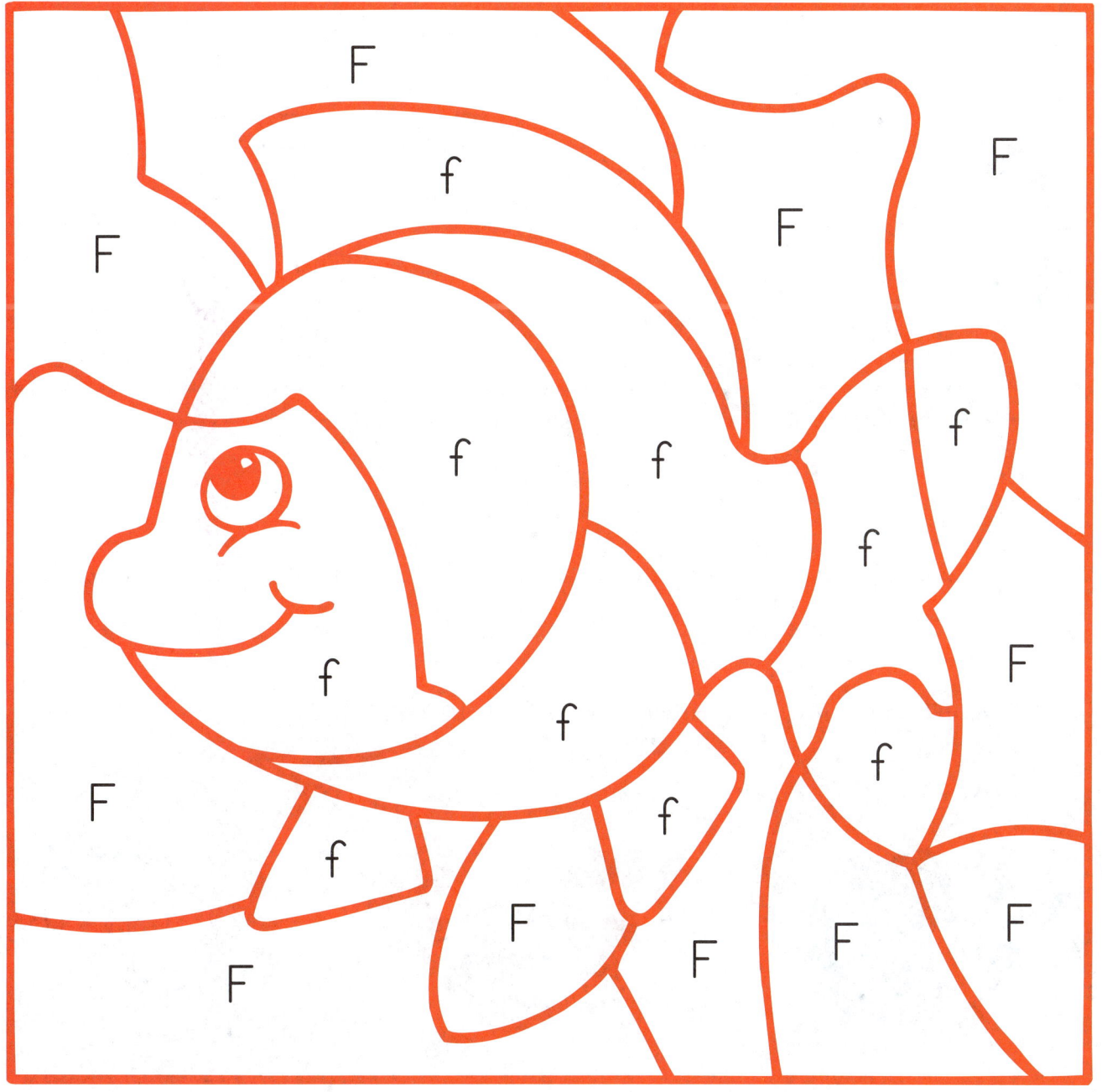

17

Ff

Directions: Trace and write the letters. Use the blank line for extra practice.

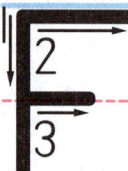

These words start with the letter **f**. Write **f** on the lines.

  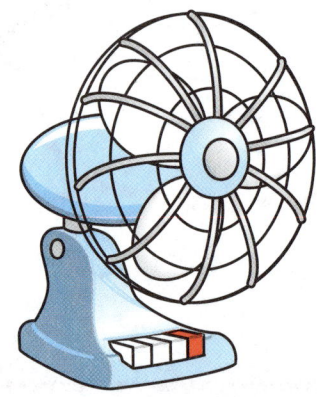

___ish   ___ox   ___an

Matching Pictures with the Sounds of D and F

Directions: Cut apart the pictures. Place the pictures that start with **Dd** on the door. Place the pictures that start with **Ff** on the fence.

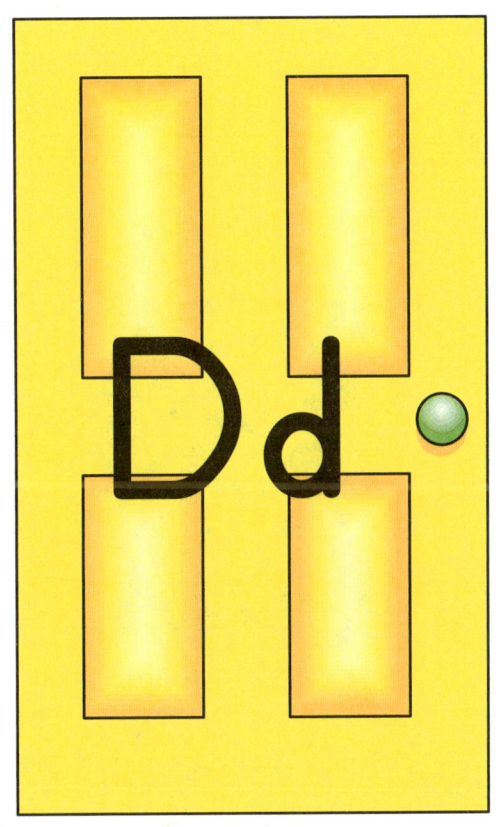

G Is for Gift

Directions: Color the spaces with **G** yellow. Color the spaces with **g** blue.

21

Gg

Directions: Trace and write the letters. Use the blank line for extra practice.

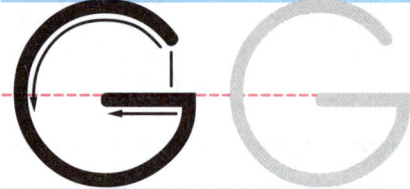

These words start with the letter **g**. Write **g** on the lines.

___oat   ___irl   ___uitar

H Is for House

Directions: Color the spaces with H red. Color the spaces with h blue.

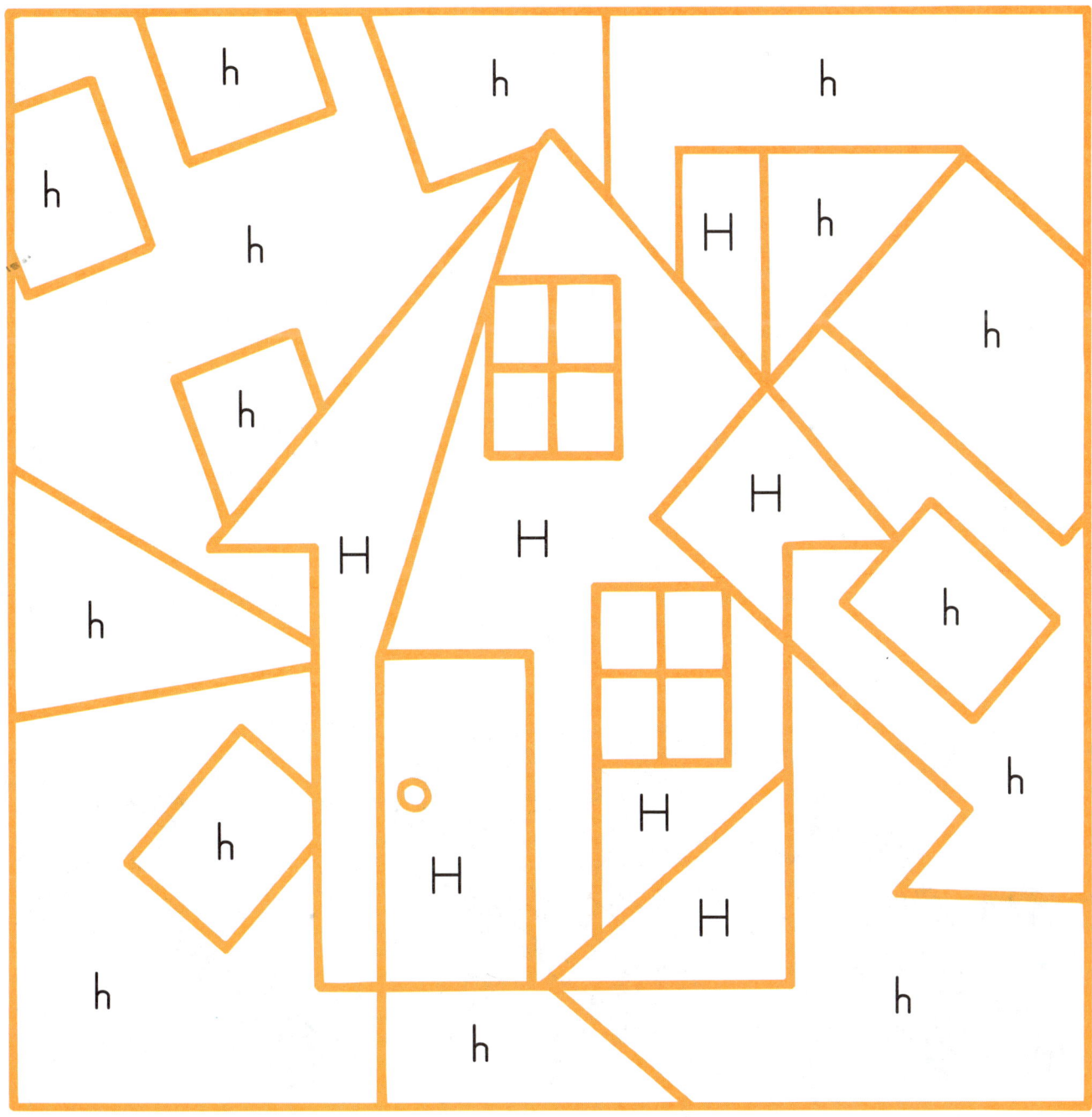

Hh

Directions: Trace and write the letters. Use the blank line for extra practice.

These words start with the letter **h**. Write **h** on the lines.

   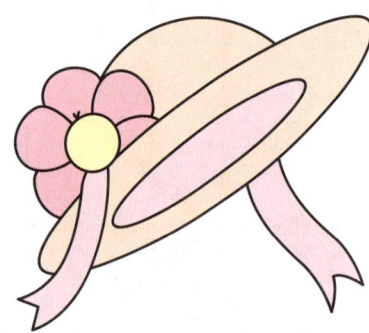   

___orse   ___at   ___ammer

Matching Pictures with the Sounds of G and H

Directions: Cut apart the pictures. Place the pictures that start with **Gg** on the game. Place the pictures that start with **Hh** on the heart.

I Is for Ice Cream

Directions: Color the spaces with I pink. Color the spaces with i yellow.

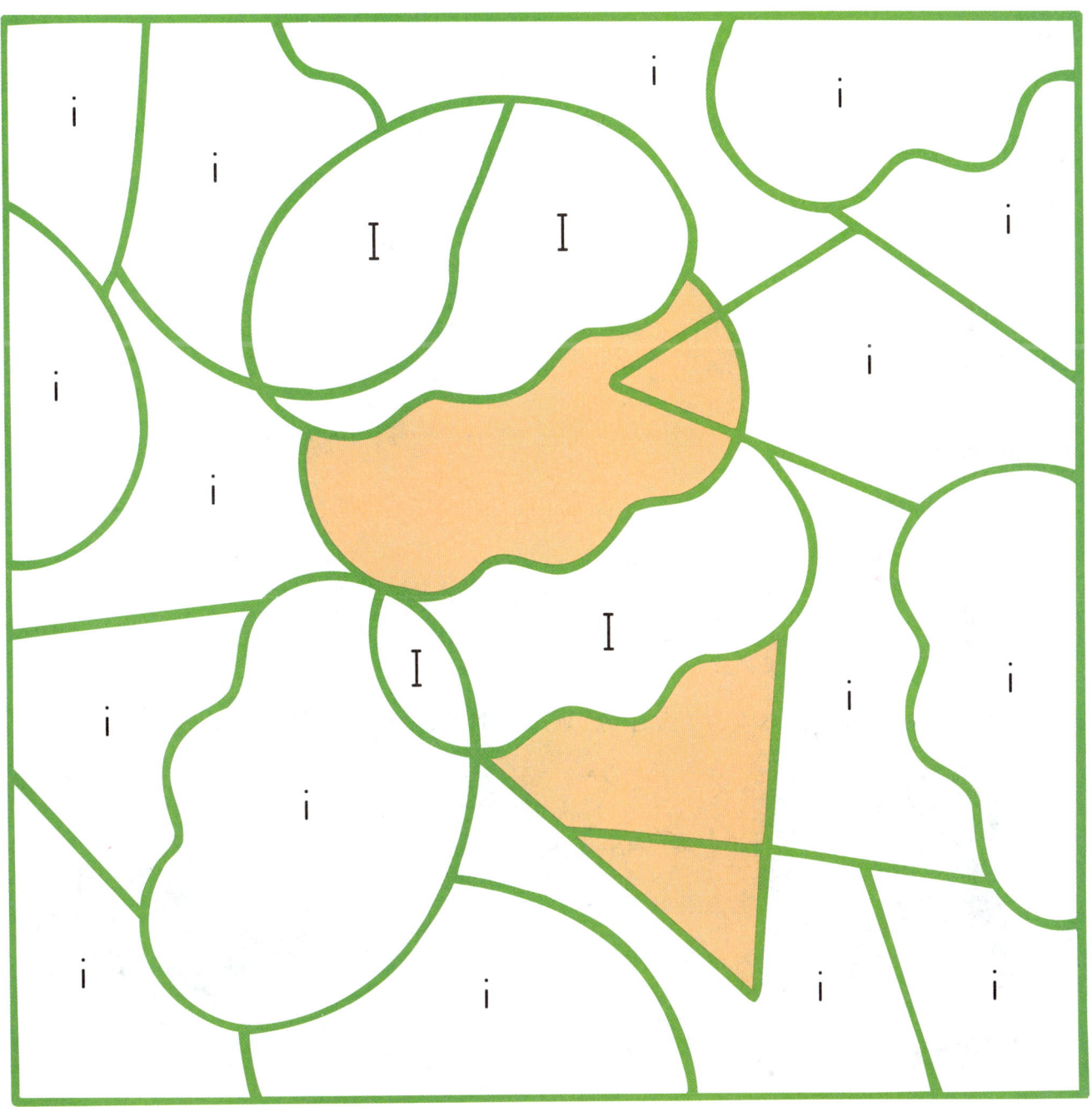

Ii

Directions: Trace and write the letters. Use the blank line for extra practice.

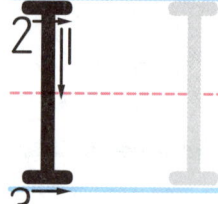

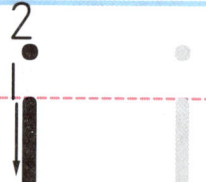

These words have the short **i** sound. Write the letter **i** on the lines.

 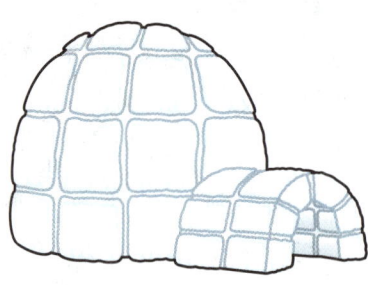 

s__x   __gloo   f__sh

J Is for Jellyfish

Directions: Color the spaces with J purple. Color the spaces with j yellow.

Jj

Directions: Trace and write the letters. Use the blank line for extra practice.

These words start with the letter **j**. Write **j** on the lines.

___et   ___am   ___ug

K Is for Kangaroo

Directions: Color the spaces with K brown. Color the spaces with k blue.

Kk

Directions: Trace and write the letters. Use the blank line for extra practice.

These words start with the letter **k**. Write **k** on the lines.

___ing   ___ite   ___ey

Matching Pictures with the Sounds of J and K

Directions: Cut apart the pictures. Place the pictures that start with **Jj** on the jar. Place the pictures that start with **Kk** on the kite.

L Is for Ladybug

Directions: Color the spaces with L black. Color the spaces with l red.

Ll

Directions: Trace and write the letters. Use the blank line for extra practice.

These words start with the letter **l**. Write **l** on the lines.

___ion ___amp ___ock

M Is for Mouse

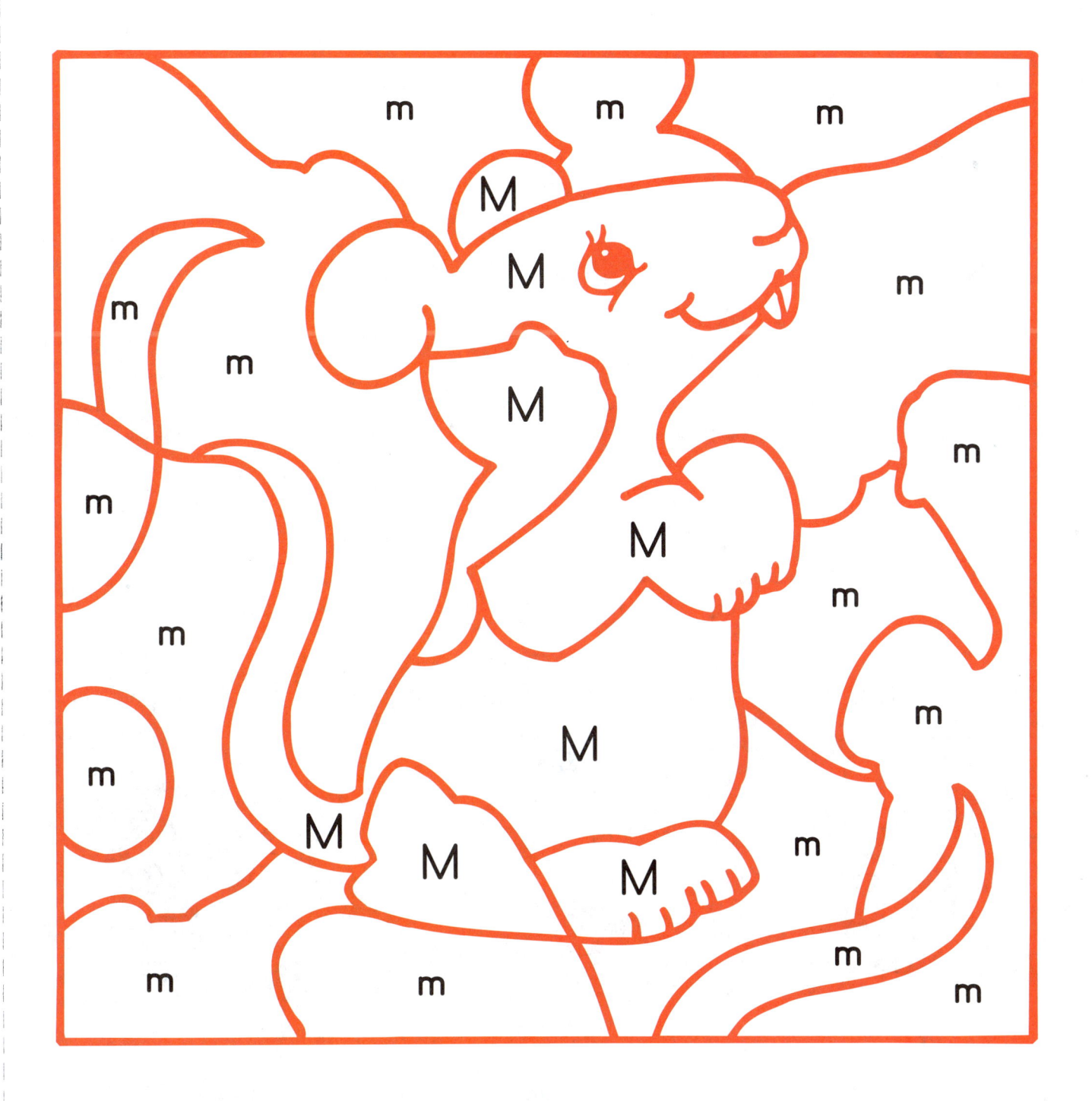

Directions: Color the spaces with **M** brown. Color the spaces with **m** green.

37
© Carson-Dellosa

Mm

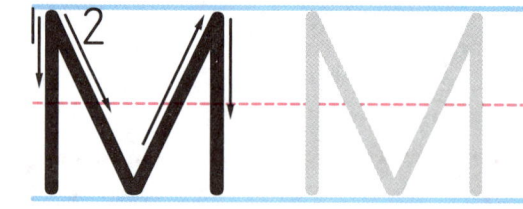

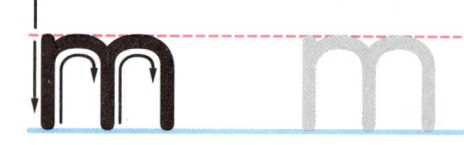

Directions: Trace and write the letters. Use the blank line for extra practice.

M M

m m

These words start with the letter **m**. Write **m** on the lines.

___ask    ___ilk    ___ouse

Matching Pictures with the Sounds of L and M

Directions: Cut apart the pictures. Place the pictures that start with **Ll** on the leaf. Place the pictures that start with **Mm** on the moon.

cut

N Is for Newt

Directions: Color the spaces with N black. Color the spaces with n yellow.

41

© Carson-Dellosa

Nn

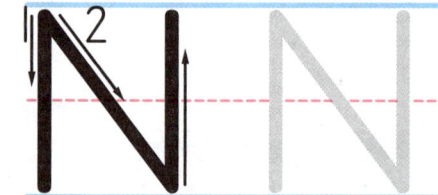

Directions: Trace and write the letters. Use the blank line for extra practice.

N N

n n

These words start with the letter **n**. Write **n** on the lines.

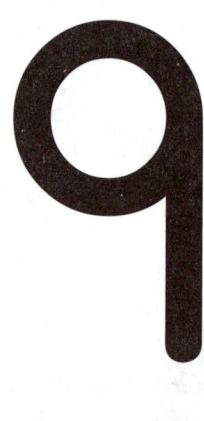

___est   ___ail   ___ine

42
© Carson-Dellosa

O Is for Octopus

Directions: Color the spaces with O orange. Color the spaces with o pink.

Oo

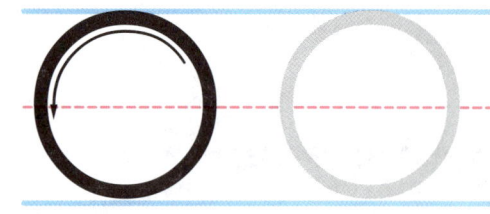

Directions: Trace and write the letters. Use the blank line for extra practice.

These words have the letter **o**. Write **o** on the lines.

___ctopus   ___strich   ___veralls

P Is for Penguin

Directions: Color the spaces with P black. Color the spaces with p gray.

45

Pp

Directions: Trace and write the letters. Use the blank line for extra practice.

P P

p p

These words start with the letter **p**. Write **p** on the lines.

___ie   ___aint   ___umpkin

Matching Pictures with the Sounds of N and P

Directions: Cut apart the pictures. Place the pictures that start with **Nn** on the nut. Place the pictures that start with **Pp** on the paper.

Nn

Pp

cut

47

© Carson-Dellosa

Q Is for Quail

Directions: Color the spaces with Q black. Color the spaces with q brown.

Qq

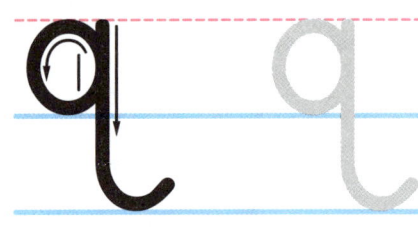

Directions: Trace and write the letters. Use the blank line for extra practice.

These words start with the letter **q**. Write **q** on the lines.

___uilt   ___ueen   ___uail

R Is for Rabbit

Directions: Color the spaces with R brown. Color the spaces with r yellow.

Rr

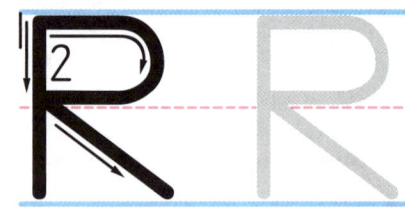

Directions: Trace and write the letters. Use the blank line for extra practice.

R R

r r

These words start with the letter **r**. Write **r** on the lines.

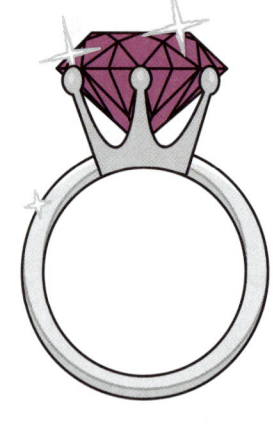

___ope   ___ing   ___abbit

S Is for Sun

Directions: Color the spaces with S yellow. Color the spaces with s blue.

© Carson-Dellosa

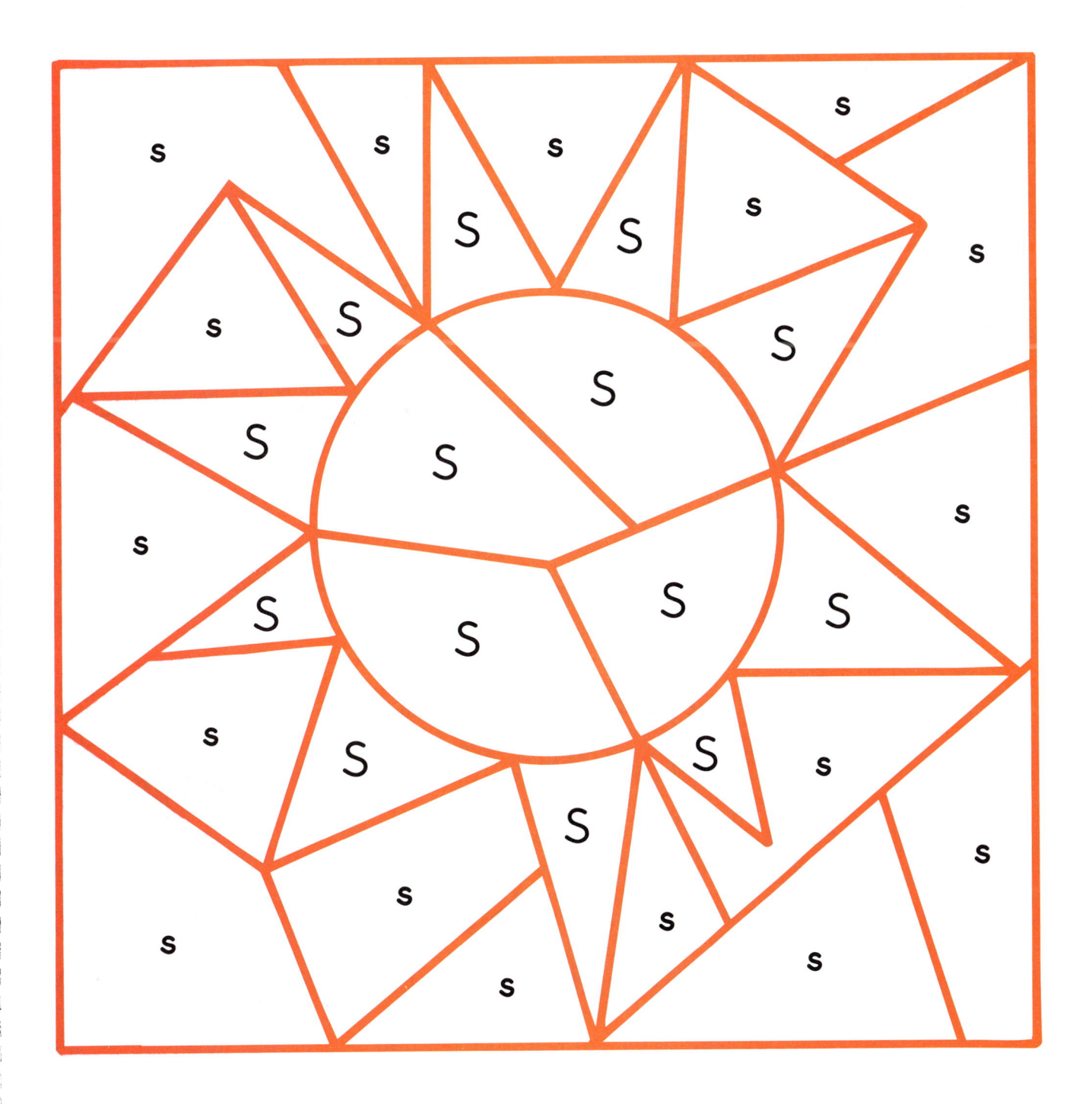

53

Ss

Directions: Trace and write the letters. Use the blank line for extra practice.

S S

s s

These words start with the letter **s**. Write **s** on the lines.

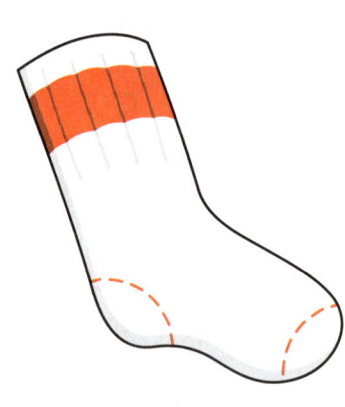

___aw   ___ock   ___even

Matching Pictures with the Sounds of R and S

Directions: Cut apart the pictures. Place the pictures that start with **Rr** on the rocket. Place the pictures that start with **Ss** on the sailboat.

cut

55

T Is for Turtle

Directions: Color the spaces with T brown. Color the spaces with t yellow.

57

© Carson-Dellosa

Tt

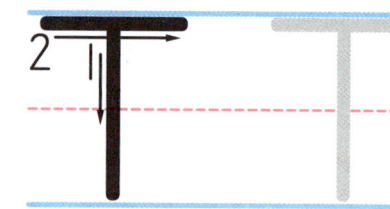

Directions: Trace and write the letters. Use the blank line for extra practice.

These words start with the letter **t**. Write **t** on the lines.

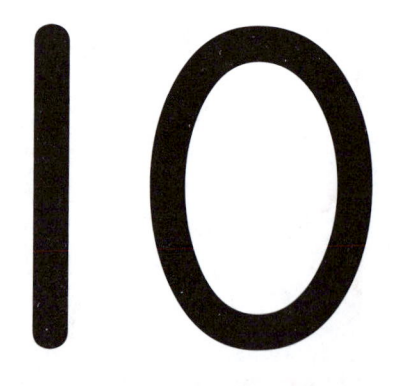

___op   ___urtle   ___en

U Is for Umbrella

Directions: Color the spaces with U red. Color the spaces with u blue.

Uu

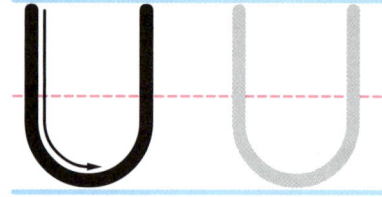

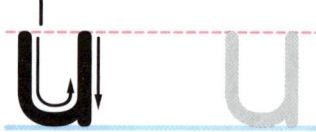

Directions: Trace and write the letters. Use the blank line for extra practice.

U U

u u

These words have the letter **u**. Write **u** on the lines.

___mbrella    ___nicorn    ___nicycle

V Is for Vulture

Directions: Color the spaces with V black. Color the spaces with v gray.

Vv

Directions: Trace and write the letters. Use the blank line for extra practice.

These words start with the letter **v**. Write **v** on the lines.

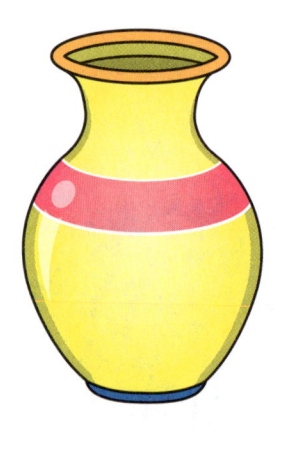

___ase    ___est    ___acuum

Matching Pictures with the Sounds of T and V

Directions: Cut apart the pictures. Place the pictures that start with **Tt** on the tent. Place the pictures that start with **Vv** on the van.

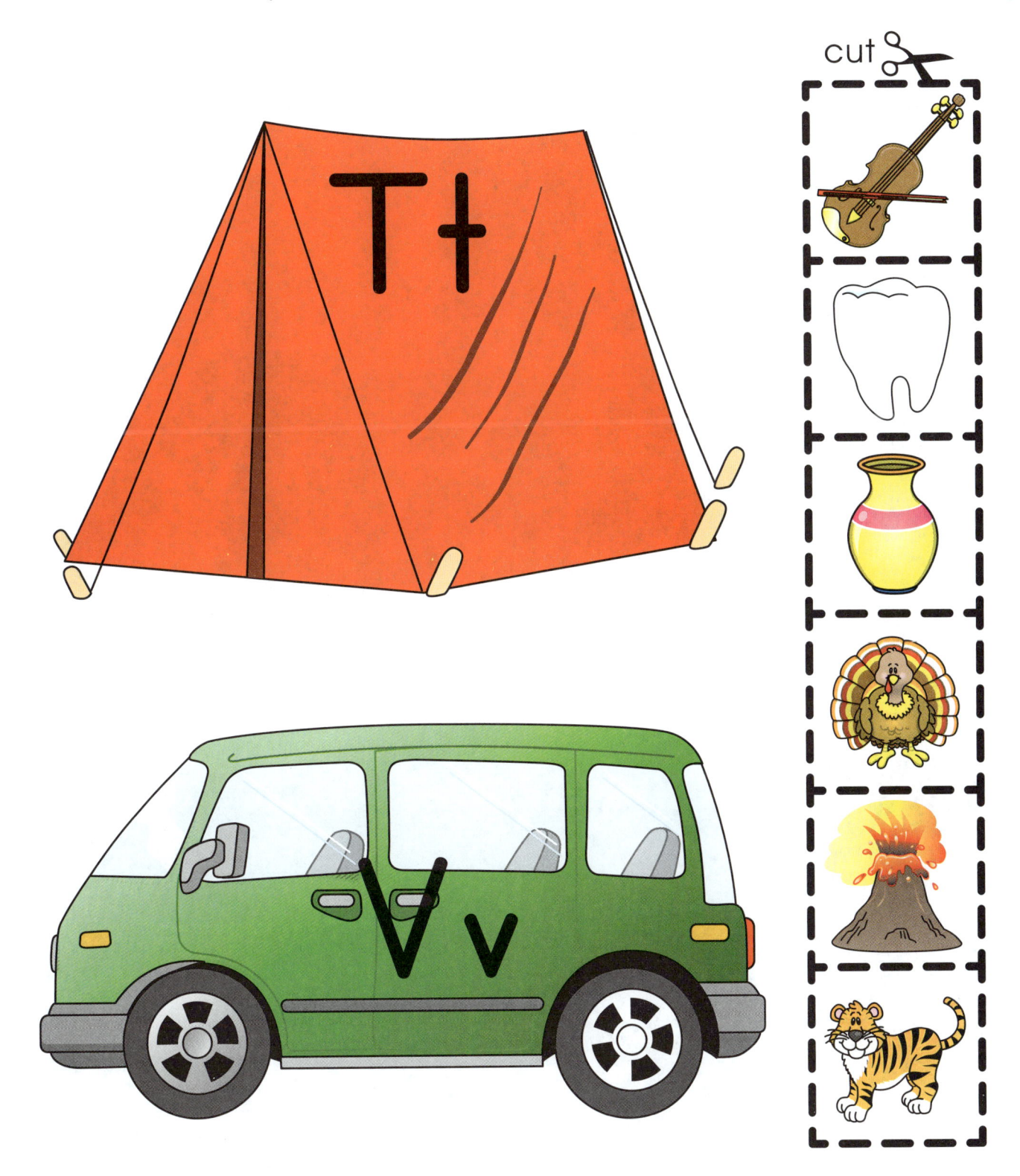

63

© Carson-Dellosa

W Is for Walrus

Directions: Color the spaces with **W** brown. Color the spaces with **w** blue.

Ww

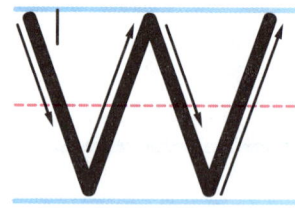

Directions: Trace and write the letters. Use the blank line for extra practice.

W W

w w

These words start with the letter **w**. Write **w** on the lines.

___eb ___atch ___agon

66
© Carson-Dellosa

X Is for Fox

Directions: Color the spaces with X orange. Color the spaces with x green.

Xx

Directions: Trace and write the letters. Use the blank line for extra practice.

These words have the letter **x**. Write **x** on the lines.

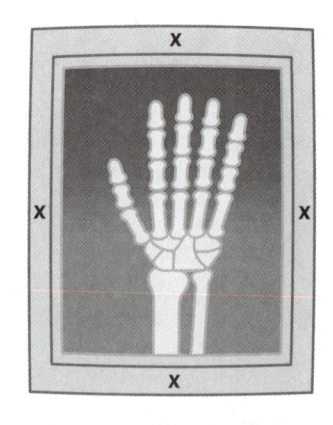

___-ray

bo___

fo___

Y Is for Yak

Directions: Color the spaces with Y black. Color the spaces with y brown.

Yy

Directions: Trace and write the letters. Use the blank line for extra practice.

Y Y

y y

These words start with the letter **y**. Write **y** on the lines.

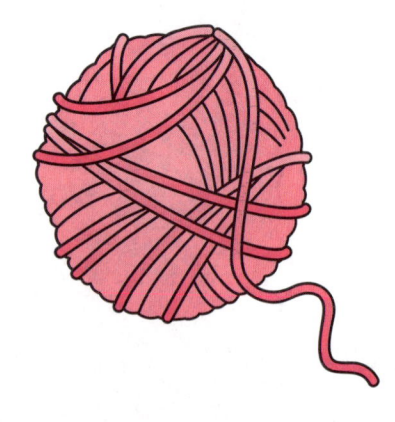

___ak ___arn ___o-yo

Z Is for Zebra

Directions: Color the spaces with Z black. Color the spaces with z green.

Zz

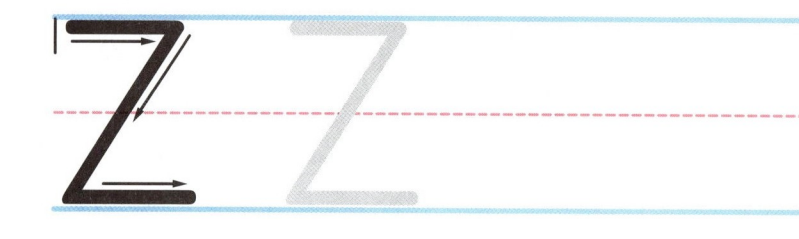

Directions: Trace and write the letters. Use the blank line for extra practice.

Z Z

z z

These words start with the letter **z**. Write **z** on the lines.

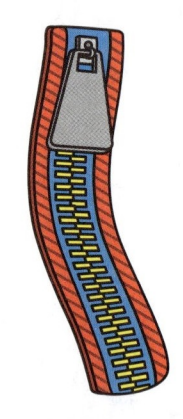

___ebra   ___ipper   ___oo

Matching Pictures with the Sounds of W, Y, and Z

Directions: Cut apart the pictures. Place the pictures that start with **Ww** on the window. Place the pictures that start with **Yy** on the yarn. Place the pictures that start with **Zz** on the zero.

cut

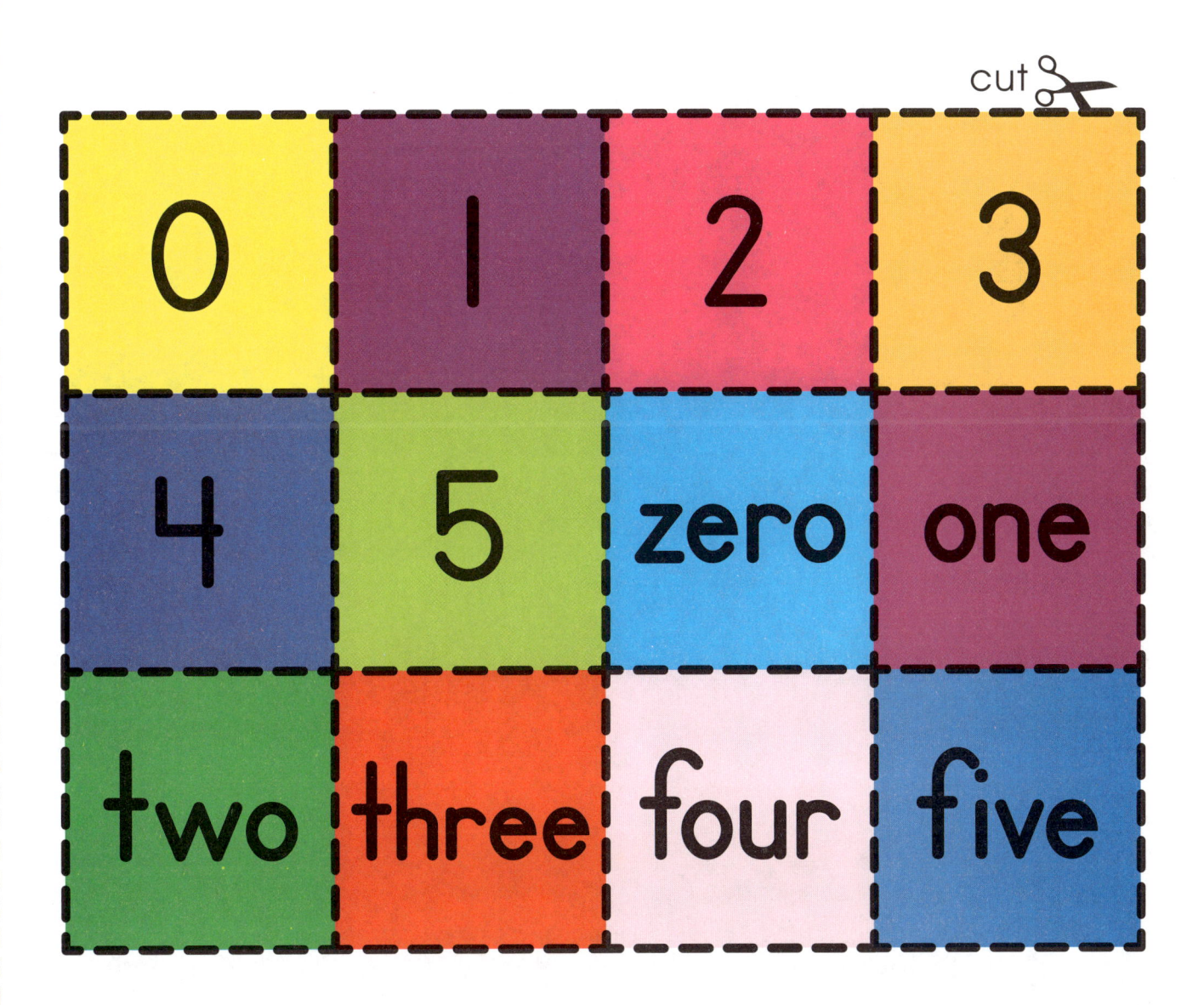

Word and Number Matching Game

Directions: Cut apart the cards. Match the number words to the numbers.

cut ✂

0	1	2	3
4	5	zero	one
two	three	four	five

Color Matching Game

Directions: Cut apart the cards. Match the color words to the crayons.

cut

red	orange	yellow	green
blue	purple	brown	black

© Carson-Dellosa

All About Me

Directions: Fill in the spaces to make a flyer about yourself. You might like to give it to your teacher on the first day of school.

My name is _____

My birthday is _____

I am _____ **years old.**

My address is _____

My phone number is _____